CHINS AND NEEDLES

ANDY DONATO

CHINS AND NEEDLES

Political Cartoons

KEY PORTER·BOOKS

Canadian Cataloguing in Publication Data
Donato, Andy, 1937-
    Chins and Needles

ISBN 1-55013-009-9

1. World politics — 1985-1995 — Caricatures and
cartoons. 2. Canada — Politics and government —
1984-   — Caricatures and cartoons.*
3. Canadian wit and humor, Pictorial. I. Title.

NC1449.D66A4 1986   741.5'971   C86-094489-1

A collection of cartoons which appeared
in **The Toronto Sun**.

Key Porter Books Limited
70 The Esplanade
Toronto, Ontario
Canada   M5E 1R2

Design: *First Image*
Printing and Binding: *Webcom Ltd.*
Printed and bound in Canada

86 87 88 89   6 5 4 3 2 1

INTRODUCTION

Editorial cartooning is, of course, the blackest of the medieval arts.

More sinister than newt-soup-making, tougher than bringing up the beyond in a crystal ball, drawing an editorial cartoon is — some say — the most sophisticated form of The Curse. We're talking art voodoo, the devil drawing with pins in it. Booga booga.

Kings, queens and first ministers have always twitched horribly when they saw themselves as cartoon wizards saw them. Then they sent their executive assistant over with $500 to buy the original drawing for the office wall. It's magic.

All your wizards, your witches, tried their hand at editorial cartooning. It was fun. Profitable. Spooky.

Merlin, the witches in Macbeth, The Wicked Witch of the West in Oz, they all had the big 96-color box of Crayolas as kids. They could say Chartreuse and Burnt Sienna and Cinnamon before you and your sister could say Mom. These wizard cartoonists never wanted a bike; they wanted a selection of felt-tip pens and a jumbo tube of cadmium yellow. So did Donato.

But we live in surprisingly wizardless times.

I blame it on the good wizard called Shazam. Remember him? The wizard Shazam lived on a mist-shrouded mountain in Captain Marvel comics; no coincidence, this continuing connection between wizards and pop art. The wiz befriended a little lame city kid, became his all-powerful protector.

Whenever little Billy Batson — a *newsboy* for Pete's sake! — when Billy would get beaten up by bullies or slugged silly by comic strip thugs, he had only to say "Shazam!"

The mere mention of Shazam's name brought a flash of lightning, a clap of thunder and ZAP! — there was superhero Captain Marvel, the mightily-muscled protector of the pounded-upon. You show me a kid who couldn't have used that thunderclap, that big guy with fists like hams four, maybe five days a week.

But that comic strip brought chaos.

You had millions of kids in their backyards, screaming "Shazam!" And like a bad rural phone line, like too many terminals on a computer system that crashes, all those kids dissipated the wizard Shazam's power. He couldn't help *any* of us. The word didn't work.

We terrified tots were thus condemned to be beaten forever with our own saxophone cases in the schoolyard. "Shazam!" we would wail — 'til a fistful of fingers closed each mouth for the afternoon.

A lot of us lost faith in wizards.

We learned to live with bullies and boobs and bad apples. We assumed it was part of growing up.

But one of the first afternoons I ever worked at the Toronto *Sun*, I witnessed the most curious thing.

It was mid-afternoon. The editors were slow coming back from lunch. The SUNshine girl for the next day's paper was not as good-looking as my sister. The marvel-and-mayhem barometer was reading "Low" — bad news for a morning tabloid. Even the Dr. Lamb column was about hangnails. Yeesh. The photo desk was offering people asleep on park benches as a possible color front. It was what you might call your Slow Day. How fast that all changed.

"Donato!" an hysterical voice yells. It's always the editor. (John Downing, Barbara Amiel, Peter Worthington, all the editors have screamed the word the same way. Billy Batson would have screamed it that way too. And the effect is always the same.)

There is a rumble outside the *Sun* building on King Street — but no trolleycar goes by. There is a blinding flash of light and the computer system crashes.

Then the elevator doors open and — fresh from some mist-shrouded mountaintop — a beaming Andy Donato appears. Sometimes there is a supernatural glow, an aura, around his nattily-dressed figure. Sometimes the art cardboard he carries under his arm is still damp.

He walks through the city room with his usual Bugs Bunny grin. Women swoon. Reporters care not that the computer crash has sent their copy straight to Hades. Photographers stop fudging their mileage claims. The wiz has arrived. He carries the thunderbolt under his arm. Everything is going to be All Right. Tomorrow's paper is going to be Okay.

Donato has been described over the years as (choose one) a roly-poly Renaissance man, one of those flat-footed rubber clowns that teeter when you hit it, Michelangelo's plucky brother Micheldonato, or a cross between a Cabbage Patch doll and the Pillsbury Doughboy. Honest! That's what other writers have tagged him with. You can see how confused he has them; the power to cloud men's minds so they cannot truly see him. Most women prefer to think of him as the adorable and witty Canadian panda, Ursus Donatosus. He is — they tell me — well off the Hugability Meter.

A smiling Donato strides to the frightened editor's

side. Then he tosses down the next day's lightning bolt, disproving the adage that lightning never strikes twice. Donato hits the same space with the same sizzling zap every day of the week. The odds against this phenomenon are astronomical.

It is the most-read-thing in the paper. It keeps people from looking at the not-so-hot SUNshine girl or muttering "Page Six is a little slow today." And on those days when the world is very dark indeed, when you would think it hard to produce *anything*, Donato delivers the best quicker than Pizza Pizza.

Connoisseurs and commoners will instantly recall images for Donato's Diefenbaker-Pearson flag debate cartoons; Richard Nixon in Pinocchio kneepants, his nose growing with each Watergate lie; the flap-eared beagle dog lying on a pair of boots the day that Lyndon Johnson died; or his award-winning *American Dream*, a celebrated 1980 vision of Marines planting a flag on (and up) Iran's Ayatollah Khomeini.

From his first art job lettering a truck for $2.50, to being seriously under-appreciated as a fledgling newspaper cartoonist, to his present status as Giant of Journalism and lint-picker to presidents and publishers, Donato perhaps deserves a paragraph. This is that paragraph.

You already know he is a wizard, at the world-class level of cartoon loons able to puncture the pompous, and detail the deadly happenings of the day. Today and tomorrow, week after week, ZAP!

So Donato once forgot how to spell his own name on a cartoon. Lucky for him nobody at the *Sun* knew anybody called DANTO.

So he has a hard time drawing people sitting with their legs crossed. ("It's tough to get the way their pants fold," he says.)

Take a peek at any cartoon in this book. They're all signed with the right name. And nobody has their legs crossed.

Gary Dunford

RETURN OF THE RAINMAKER

PITCHING TUESDAY, SEPTEMBER 4.

BRIAN 'BEAN BALL' MULDOON
* *BAIE COMEAU BUCKS*
FIRST REAL YEAR PITCHING IN MAJORS. RIGHT-HANDER WHO TENDS TO FALL OFF MOUND TO LEFT AFTER PITCH. GETS CHUMMY WITH PRESS THEN REGRETS IT. THROWS A LOT OF PITCHES BUT RARELY IN STRIKE ZONE. FAVORITE PITCH IS THE BLARNEY BALL.

JOHN 'RAPID FIRE' BURNER
* *QUADRA QUACKERS*
PITCHED IN MAJORS IN '75. LEFT AFTER DISPUTE WITH MANAGER. TRYING TO MAKE COME BACK. RIGHT-HANDER, NOW THROWING LEFT. LIKES TO SLAP FELLOW PLAYERS ON BACK SIDE. HABIT THAT ONCE HURT HIS THROWING ARM. LICKS LIPS A LOT. UMPS ALWAYS CHECKING FOR SPIT BALLS.

ED 'LEFTY' BROADBAT
* *OSHAWA SOCIALS*
VETERAN PITCHER. THROWS SINKERS, SLIDERS FASTBALLS, CURVES AND KNUCKLE BALLS. NEVER ARGUES WITH UMPS, UMPS NEVER ARGUE WITH HIM. HAS NEVER WON A GAME. NEVER WILL WIN A GAME.

DONATO
TORONTO SUN

SPINE OF STEEL

DONATO *TORONTO SUN*

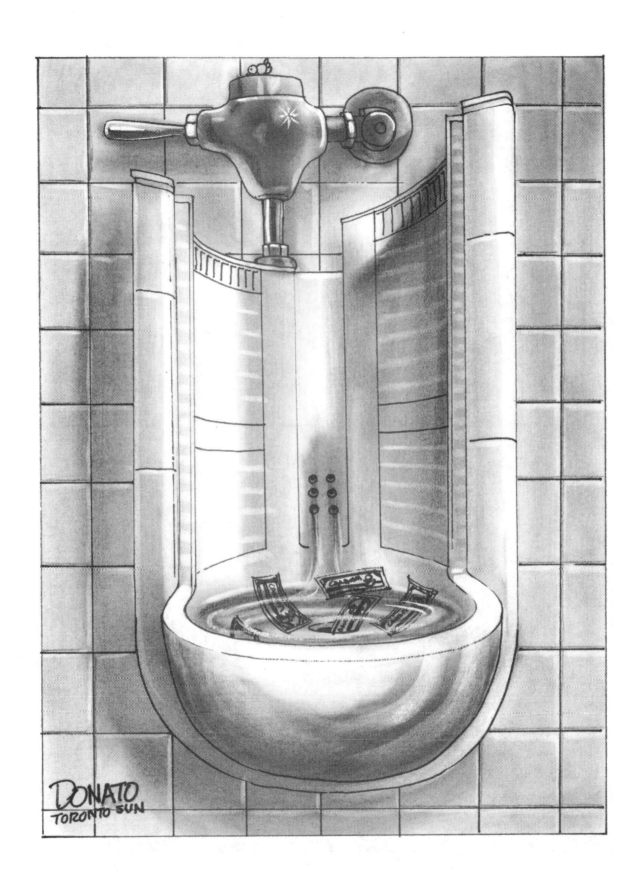

DONATO
TORONTO SUN

PREMIER RICHARD BTFSPLK

TINY TALENT TIME

DONATO
TORONTO SUN

DONATO
TORONTO SUN

ALL IN THE FAMILY WITH CROSBIE, FRILLS AND CASH

DONATO
TORONTO SUN

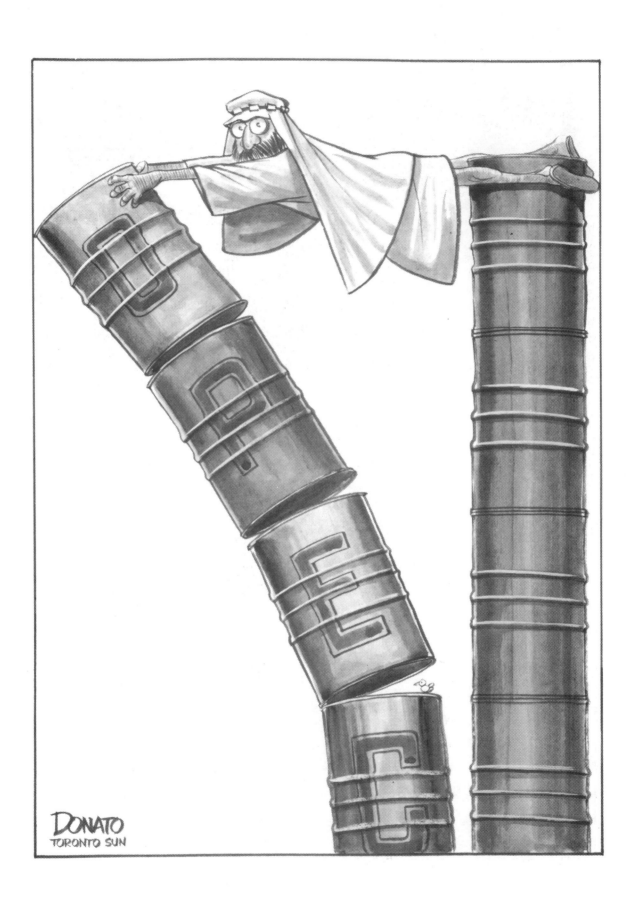

TUNNEL TALK

ONTARIO LIBERAL CAUCUS

NEWFOUNDLAND
by John Crosbie

DONATO
TORONTO SUN

FREE TRADE

DONATO
TORONTO SUN

CANADIAN EMBASSY-MOSCOW

AGENT DOUBLE OH, DOUBLE OH, WE'VE JUST BEEN INFORMED THE KGB IS USING A SPECIAL *SPRAY* ON OUR PEOPLE!

THEY'RE SPRAYING THINGS LIKE DOOR KNOBS AND STEERING WHEELS AND IT ENABLES THEM TO TRACK OUR AGENTS! TO AVOID BEING TRACKED ON YOUR NEXT ASSIGNMENT...

...I WANT YOU TO WASH WITH THIS SPECIAL SOAP, THEN CHANGE INTO THESE CLOTHES WE KNOW ARE CLEAN AND SAFE!

NOW, WHAT EVER YOU DO, *DON'T* TOUCH ANYTHING THAT COULD BE *SPRAYED!*

DONATO TORONTO SUN

DONATO
TORONTO SUN

...AND THE FARMER'S DAUGHTER

TINY PERFECT PREMIER

DONATO
TORONTO SUN

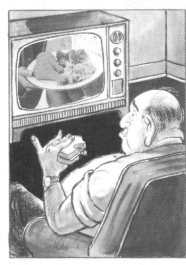

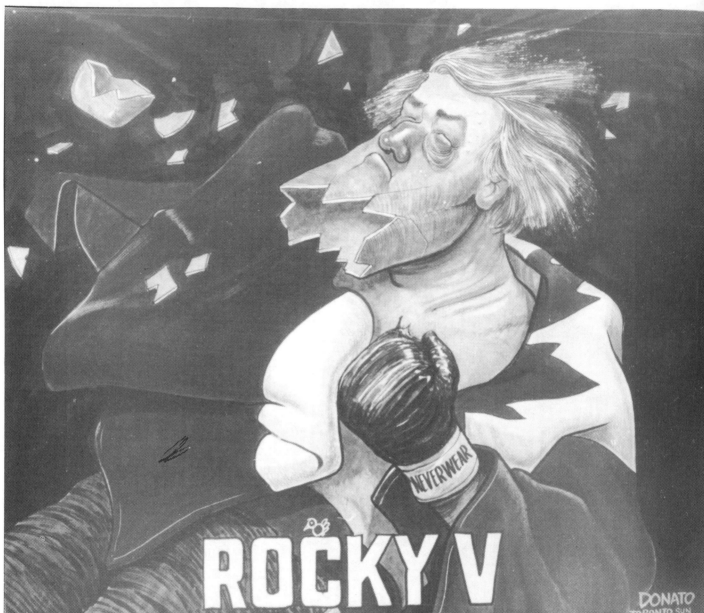

ROCKY V

DONATO
TORONTO SUN

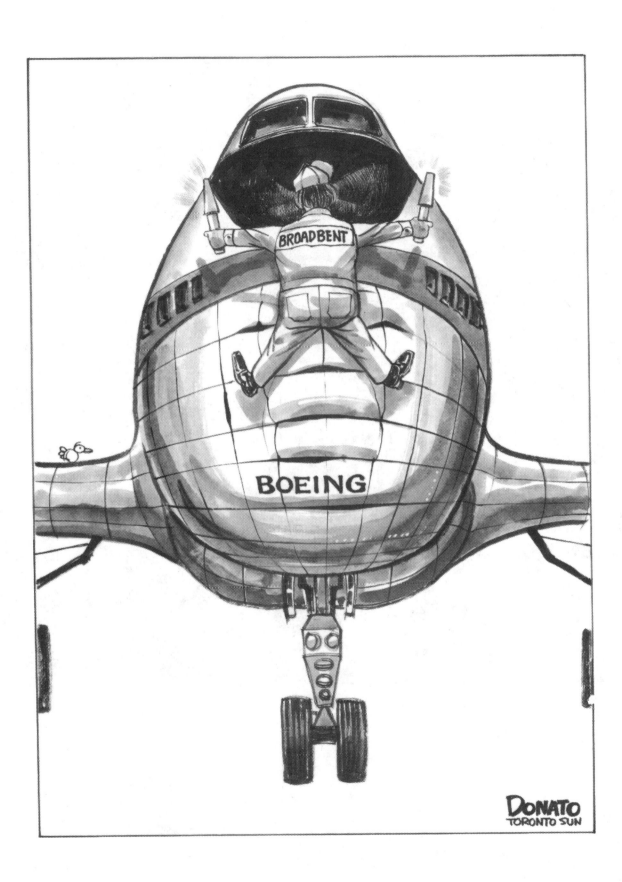

BANK

PATRONAGE

33rd PARLIAMENT

DONATO TORONTO SUN

"Somebody walks by an open window, apparently, and hears himself and his family being savaged and his reputation being attacked. I suppose you would have to not be human not to listen."

Brian Mulroney, February 1, 1986.

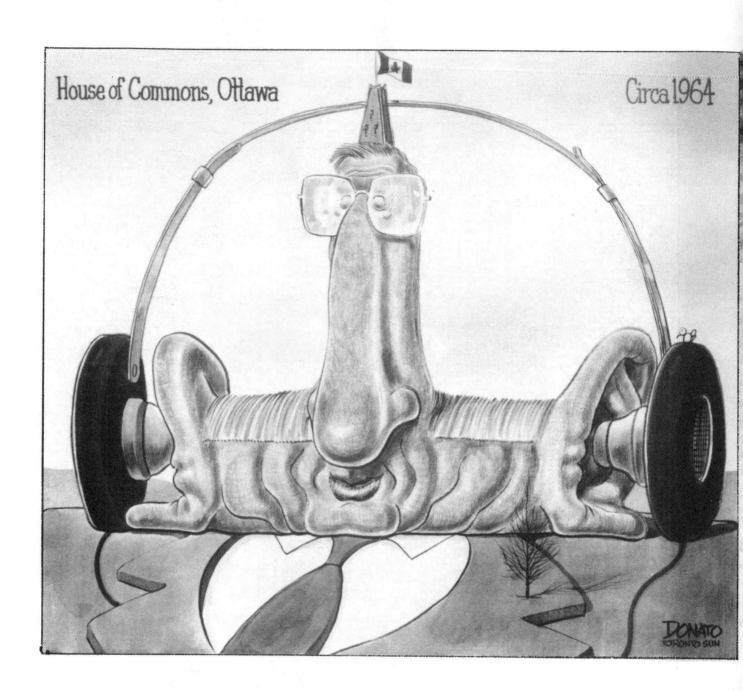

NEW ISSUE

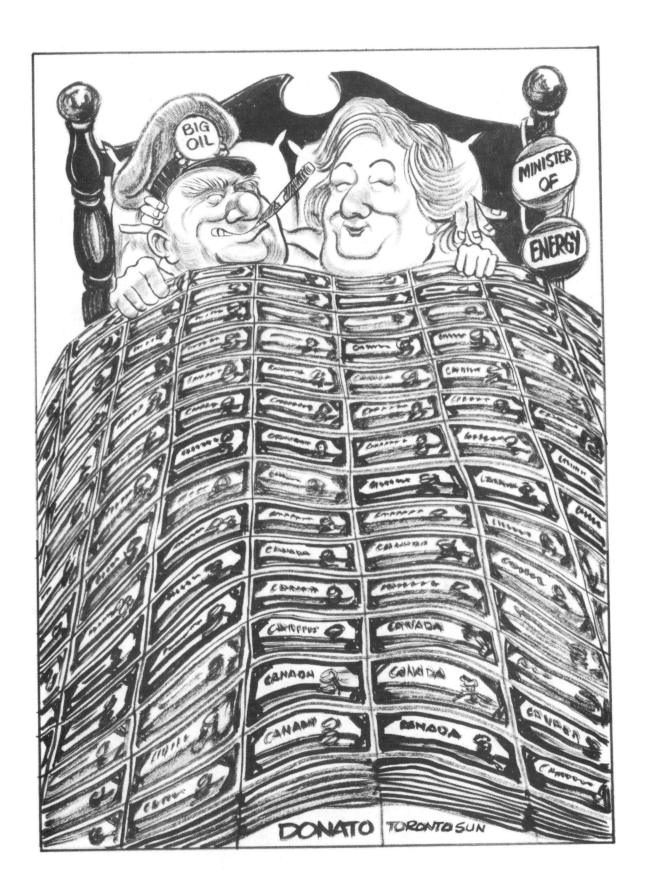

DONATO
TORONTO SUN

DONATO TORONTO SUN

SPENDING SOCKS

REVENUE SHOES

DONATO
TORONTO SUN

DONATO *TORONTO SUN*

"THE PARTY IS UNITED BEHIND ME!"

1976

1986

DONATO
TORONTO SUN

WINNER OF THE 1986
KHADAFY AWARD
FOR BEST DEFENDER
IN A PEACEFUL
NAVIGATION
EXERCISE

DONATO *TORONTO SUN*

BLIND TRUST

DONATO TORONTO SUN

BLIND JUSTICE

MINISTER OF JUSTICE

DONATO
TORONTO SUN

DONATO

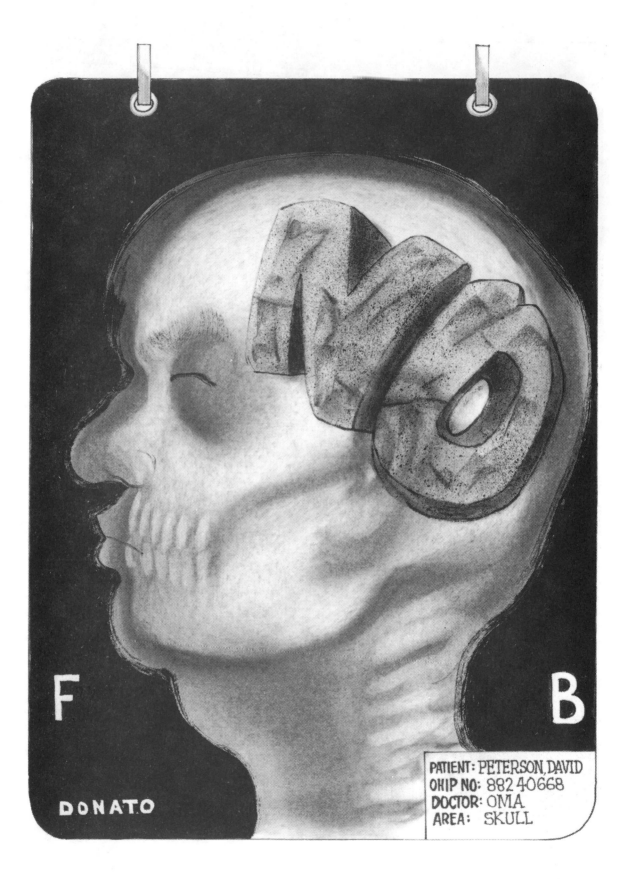

F

B

DONATO

PATIENT: PETERSON, DAVID
OHIP NO: 882 40668
DOCTOR: OMA
AREA: SKULL

DONATO
TORONTO SUN

CLASSIFIEDS

COMPANIONS

Married couple, one in politics one in business would like to meet couple with similar interests. Write with photos to: S. Stevens Parliament Hill, Ottawa, Ont.

Married couple, one in politics one in business would like to meet couple with similar interests Write with photo to E. Caplan Queen's Park, Toronto, Ont.

DONATO TORONTO SUN

SUBSCRIBE TODAY

TO CANADA'S MOST COLORFUL MAGAZINE

16 PAGES, 17 FULL COLOR PHOTOS OF BRIAN MULRONEY! DISCOVER LIFE WITH THE BEAUTIFUL PEOPLE! WHAT THEY DRINK AND EAT... HOW THEY DRESS!

◀ BONUS!

*BE ONE OF THE FIRST 25,000,000 SUBSCRIBERS AND YOU WILL RECEIVE **FREE** THIS FOUR HOUR VIDEO TAPE OF **THE LIFE OF BRIAN!***

PLUS THIS PHOTO ALBUM

CONTAINING FULL COLOR PHOTOS OF BRIAN WITH HIS FILM CREW, HAIRDRESSER TAILOR AND MAKEUP MAN!

EXTRA! ORDER THE JUNE

ISSUE OF 'CANADA TODAY' <u>ONLY</u> AND YOU WILL RECEIVE A FULL COLOR POSTER OF A HERCULES AIRCRAFT BEING LOADED WITH BRIAN'S LUGGAGE FOR HIS TRIP TO NEW YORK!

DONATO TORONTO SUN